WATER PLANET

ARROWHEAD BOOKS

WATER PLANET

Ralph Fletcher

ARROWHEAD BOOKS

PUBLISHED BY ARROWHEAD BOOKS,

A DIVISION OF

LANGUAGE FOR LEARNING ASSOCIATES

3 GERRISH DRIVE

DURHAM, NEW HAMPSHIRE 03824

INTERNATIONAL STANDARD BOOK NUMBER

0-9628238-5-6

THANKS TO DREW LAMM, BILL MARTIN, JR., CYN-
THIA RYLANT, ELISABETH VOIGT, SUSANNAH
VOIGT, AND JANE YOLEN, WHOSE COMMENTS
AND SUGGESTIONS HELPED SHAPE THE POEMS IN
THIS COLLECTION. THANKS TO WAYNE GLUSKER
FOR USE OF HIS PHOTOGRAPH ON THE COVER,
AND TO JERRY KELLY FOR HIS PAINSTAKING
WORK BRINGING THIS BOOK INTO THE WORLD.
THANKS, ALWAYS, TO JOANN.

For the best
short poem of all:

Taylor
Adam
Robert
and Joseph

INVITATION

When I was a kid, we had a freak hail storm on the Fourth Of July. The storm started a chain reaction in our house: it pushed in a window screen which knocked over the bird cage which killed Tweety, our parakeet. We found her lying in the cage, surrounded by melting hail pellets, which looked to me exactly how I imagined parakeet eggs might look. My brothers and sisters and I were too shocked to cry. Instead we got onto our hands and knees and gathered up all the hail pieces we could find, put them into the freezer, and tried to forget about it.

Six months later we took out the hail. The little balls were all frozen together. Seeing them reminded us of Tweety. Now we had to try very hard not to cry.

Have you ever seen bushes after an ice storm when every branch, every twig and bud, is coated with a fine layer of crystalline ice? Have you ever tasted real creek water that was clean and sweet and safe to drink? Have you ever seen a bank of fog scratching its soft belly on the top of a house? After a day at the beach, have you ever been lying in bed, nearly asleep, only to hear a strange roaring sound in your ears that gets louder and louder until a little pool of seawater that had been trapped in your ear comes spilling out onto the pillow?

Here's what I believe: if there is magic on this planet, it is a water kind of magic. I have not found anything else quite so beautiful or mysterious.

These poems celebrate water in its three basic disguises: liquid, ice and steam. Some poems have water as the main idea. Other poems mention water but are really about something else.

You will find long poems and short poems, poems that are silly, happy and sad. In Part One, "Water Songs", you'll mostly find rhyming poems that are fun to read out loud. The poems in Part Two, "Deeper Water", are a little more serious.

I'll be very surprised if you like all the poems in this book. If any poem, or part of a poem, seems hard to understand, don't worry. You can leave that part and come back to it.

Reading and rereading poems is what started me writing poetry. I'll be happy if any of these poems inspire you to write poems of your own.

I invite you to read these poems anyway you like. Read them in order or skip around. If you find a poem that grabs you, copy it down for yourself, send it to a friend, read it to a little sister or brother. Write me a letter about it. If you find a poem you really like, you could memorize it. That way, even if you lose this book, you'll have that poem forever.

Ralph Fletcher

PART ONE

WATER SONGS

H$_2$O

The recipe
      for water is
the same as
      it's always been:
two parts
      hydrogen
to one part
      oxygen.

Two to one
      that's the rule
to make a water
      molecule.

WAVES

Waves on the ocean,
Ripples on the sand,
My father calling me
With a wave of his hand.

The wavy grain of wood
And the wave in my hair;
Waves of fiery autumn leaves
Tumbling through the air.

A wave of sadness
When I think of the day
My best friend Vinnie
Moved far far away.

SKIPPING STONES

Daddy skips breakfast
Elizabeth skips rope
I skip stones

George skipped fourth grade
Brian skipped out of school
I skip stones

Flat stones sharp stones
Skinny as potato chips

     ing   wrin
Kick   up   kles

     the   smooth
On   glass   lake.

IN THE BATH

In the bath
my knees are mountains
rising from a peaceful sea

After a long soak
my fingers are raisin-wrinkled
like the fingers of an old man

When I close my eyes
I am a baby again
not even born

floating

in a warm dark womb

A RAINBOW IN ICE

I found a little rainbow
Trapped in a chunk of ice.
Iced rainbows are seldom seen:
I don't expect to find one twice.

It stayed outside my window
Where the wind would keep it cold.
There were seven strands of colors
And a tiny pot of gold.

All winter long I studied it,
How the yellow rubbed the green.
Red and indigo made bookends,
While the blue nestled in between.

I wondered where it came from
This orphan rainbow child;
And though I longed to tame it
I knew to keep it wild.

One warm March day the rainbow left,
On brilliant wings it flew.
Perhaps I'll see it, fully grown,
When summer storms pass through.

MY FRIEND'S BIG BROTHER

My friend's big brother
never asked when he borrowed
the gloves I'd just bought.
(Whether I happened
to like it or not.)

My friend's big brother
snatched up my sandwich
with a surly laugh.
(And gulped the thing down
in a bite and a half.)

My friend's big brother
had ice cube eyes
and never cared how anyone felt.
(But when someone hit *him*
you'd see the ice melt.)

WATER SEEKS ITS OWN LEVEL

"Water seeks its own level"
That's what my sister always said
Until one afternoon she took a shower
Singing like a rock and roll fool
And didn't notice her elephant feet
Clamped down over the drain so the water over-
Flowed all over the bathroom floor
Leaked through Dad's just-painted ceiling
Started a spectacular w
                       a
                       t
                       e
                       r
                       f
                       a
                       l
                       l   in the hall
And made a small lake that spilled out
Onto the front steps and t
                      r
                    i
                        c
                            k
                              l
                                e
                                  d
Down to the two rose bushes she'd forgotten
As usual
        to water.

THE MAN CLOUD

In a buzzing morning meadow
When the sun was not yet high
I saw a bearded man cloud
Walking in the sky.

My brother saw it differently,
He told me with a laugh
That what I'd seen was actually
An ice-skating giraffe.

"Can't you see the long legs gliding?
With his tall neck see him riding?
I distinctly see a white giraffe
Skating 'cross the sky."

I did not stop to disagree
Or tell him he was wrong.
I saw a walking man cloud
And wished to go along.

BABIES

Faucets drip
Pools cool
Springs bubble
Babies drool

Seas sparkle
Lakes glisten
Streams gurgle
Babies listen

Rivers rise
Flood and worse
Water falls
Babies nurse

Rain drenches
Waves crash
Water quenches
Babies splash

Ice melts
Cold creeks
Hail pelts
Babies leak

RAINSHOWER

Some need a shower
Or prefer a bubblebath
Me I'll take a rainstorm
And laugh laugh laugh

If you see me outside
Don't ask me to explain
Why all my friends have fled
While I'm still lounging in the rain

My sneakers have gone soupy
My pants are all soaked through
With raindrops skiing down my nose
My hair's a seaweed stew

Don't lend me an umbrella
Or toss a lifeguard's rope—
If you really want to help
Throw out a bar of soap!

Perhaps I'll get pneumonia
Or jungle flu—who cares?
Count up all these drops of rain
And I'm a millionaire!

Some insist on a shower
Others need a scalding bath
I'll take a rainstorm any day
And laugh laugh laugh

PART TWO

DEEPER WATER

A WRITING KIND OF DAY

It is raining today,
a writing kind of day.

Each word hits the page
like a drop in a puddle
and starts off a tiny circle

of trembling feeling

that expands from the source
and slowly fades away...

I DREAMED I WAS A RIVER

I dreamed I was a river,
now swift-running and dangerous,
now slow-lazing and silted,
my toes a thousand tributaries
trickling down from mountain snows,
my body fixed yet changing,
stretching across continents,
my mouth wide open to the ocean

I dreamed I was a drop of sweat
on a quarterback's determined brow

I dreamed myself an iceberg,
an enormous moveable mass,
home to walrus, seal, Arctic tern,
feared by warships and dogsledders,
my huge underbelly never seen
by the eye of the sun

I dreamed I was a raindrop
falling on a drought-scarred field

I dreamed myself a water creature,
my ancestors all ocean-born,
my body three quarters salt water,
alive on the only known water planet

I dreamed I was a tear
in a grown man's eye

RIVER HEART

Close to the moist bank of the creek
my brother and I enter the forest.
We hide a jug of fresh apple cider,
wedged underwater between mossy stones,
and follow the stream up forest.

Later it gets hot and we branch off
through a stand of stunted pines
with bear tracks and deer droppings.
Everything here is dark and still.
We sit down to share our only apple.
"We're lost," my little brother sighs
and tries mightily not to cry.
The trees have veins like Mom's legs,
hiding us under huge hushed skirts.
Tons of raw pine creak above us.
The wind dies and Bobby jumps up:
"I hear the river calling to us!"

Off he goes and finds the creek!
It curves and hisses and glistens,
a silver snake caressed by the sun.
We race downstream to the wet place
where the cider alone waits for us.
I lift it out, dripping, triumphant,
an icy throbbing river heart.

We drink it slowly
walking home
and I feel the river
in my bones.

FIRST SNOW

Grandma would sift in the flour;
I dissolved yeast in warm water.

She'd add milk and melted butter;
I got to pound down the dough.

Then she'd sit in her yellow chair
and the strong blue-veiny hands,

dusted with flour, born last century,
became still and silent on her lap.

A long time I waited for that
dough to rise, those fingers to stir.

I still get the sweet smell of yeast
when the year's first snow starts

sifting
        sifting
                sifting
                        down

WHITE HORSES

When the wind starts gusting up
I ride with Uncle Pat to the pier
to watch the whipped-up waves
rough up the sea far off shore.

When Pat was growing up in Ireland
he used to call them white horses,
only their necks and fine heads showing,
long manes blown fiercely back.

From the pier I pick my favorites:
sea stallions and muscular mares,
rearing
       prancing
            foaming their bits

white horses
          storm-racing across the ocean

AQUARIUM

Knife-dancing angels playfully fight.
Snails move slow and like to stop.
Guppies gaze through watery windows
Hung with curtains of swirling light.

Fish hear secrets and never tell.
They sleep and eat and keep in pairs.
They listen to me in perfect silence:
I should listen half as well.

I study my fish and they study me,
Our worlds bridged by heavy glass.
But I am dry and far too heavy:
I clomp to the kitchen gracelessly.

At times my land life seems out of whack:
No fins, no gills, with unwebbed feet.
Life on earth began in the water—
Today I believe I would gladly go back.

LIQUID HAIKU

this plate of hors d'oevres
laid out on a morning leaf
four perfect dew drops

snorkling on the reef
a city of blue minnows
rush hour round my feet

luxuriating
in a puddle of sunlight
cat soaks up the warm

MUDPUPPY PLACE

Four years ago Jimmy and I
took our Swiss Army knives
whittled sticks into tiny boats
and raced them down Sumpwam's Creek.

Three years ago Jimmy and I
built a wall at Brant Rock Beach
from seaweed, stones, driftwood,
to hold back the high tide.

Two years ago Jimmy and I
found a lizard in the mud
right behind Steve Fishman's house
and renamed the swamp Mudpuppy Place.

But last year
the signs started sprouting like weeds:

CLOSED DUE TO POLLUTION

(and they're filling in
Mudpuppy Place
to build a new supermarket)

Rivers and rainforest
Mudpuppies and beaches

If we don't speak up for them

who will?

WHERE JOHN CURTAIN DROWNED (FOR TOM)

He was a tall quiet kid,
a magician on the basketball court.
He could dribble with both hands:

I once saw him make a shot
from half court
perfect swish

but he never learned how to swim.

On my brother's boat
we sail toward the spot
where John Curtain drowned.
No buoy, no marker, nothing.

When we get near the place
I stop talking

I hold my breath

and don't breathe again
'til we've sailed safely past.

DIG DOWN DEEP

"There's water everywhere,"
Bobby used to tell me.
"It's under the mountains,
even under the deserts
if you dig down deep enough."

I didn't answer him:
he was my little brother
and I'd just let him talk.

But I learned that he was right
when Bobby died a few weeks
after his seventeenth birthday.

My mother cried that night
and every night for a solid year.

Even the old dry faces
sprouted stony tears.

HOW TO MAKE A SNOW ANGEL

Go alone or with a best friend.
Find a patch of unbroken snow.

Walk on tiptoes. Step backwards
Into your very last footprints.

Slowly sit back onto the snow.
Absolutely do not use your hands.

By now you should be lying flat
With snow fitting snug around you.

Let your eyes drink some blue sky.
Close them. Breathe normally.

Move your arms back and forth.
Concentrate. Think: snow angel.

In a minute don't be surprised
If you start feeling a little funny.

Both big and small. Warm and cold.
Your breath light as a snowflake.

Sweep your legs back and forth
But keep both eyes tightly closed.

Keep moving the arms until they
Lift, tremble, wobble or float.

Stand without using your hands.
Take time to get your balance.

Take three deep breaths.
Open your eyes.

Stretch. Float. Fly!

GREAT UNCLE BERNARD

Uncle Bernard studied birds
and lived to be ninety-eight.
Up exactly at five each morning
just like during his Army days,
he'd walked a mile into the woods
to a clean mountain spring,
drink two cups new water
while the birds played reveille,
and walk back home again.

Every day like that
thirty-nine and a half years
'til just before he died.

Uncle Bernard never married.
He fought in both world wars,
had a real bayonet in his attic
and a scar on his left thigh
that had a funny shape—
like Tennessee kissing Alaska.

The water in that spring
is still so clear and cold
it gives me a headache
when I drink a cup.

GRANDPA

Grandpa came to visit every spring.
We'd get up early, just he and I,
and sneak outside at sunrise
while diamonds danced all over the lawn.
Grandpa told me how spiders work
stringing water beads on the finest thread,
decorating their webs with morning dew,
and Grandpa never lied so I knew it was true.

In winter Grandpa took me on long walks.
We always stopped at Tolliver's barn
to pull down wicked icicle swords,
each one filled with sharp clear light,
and challenged each other to death by duel.
Grandpa explained how wind works at night
sharpening icicles long as they grow,
and Grandpa never lied so I knew it was so.

In Grandpa's study we drank hot chocolate
while he read from a book of fairy tales.
I saw on his windows the blooming frost
and asked about those delicate lines.
Grandpa told me about the winter elves
who come at dusk with magical brushes
to sketch on glass their silvery hues,
and Grandpa never lied so I knew it was true.

Once Grandpa took me ice fishing at night.
He held my hand while we crossed Spy Pond
and showed me how to cut out circles of ice.
When I asked if he still missed Grandma
fat young tears rolled down his cheeks
and I heard the ice settle and moan.
He said: "Ice this deep can talk to you,"
and Grandpa never lied so I knew it was true.

WAITING FOR THE SPLASH

Last night
after you hung up
I wrote you a poem
hoping it might change your heart.

This morning I tell myself:
Get serious, man.
Someone once compared
writing a poem
and hoping it will
change the world
to dropping rose petals
down a deep well

waiting for the splash

Ralph Fletcher lives in New Hampshire with his wife, JoAnn, and kids: Taylor, Adam, Robert and Joseph. He teaches writing to teachers and children around the country. Ralph loves babies, sports, travel, novels, spicy food, a huge crackling fire on a snowy day. He is the oldest of nine kids, an Eagle Scout, born on St. Patrick's Day. Favorite color: green.

Ralph's other books include *Walking Trees*, *What A Writer Needs,* and the collections of poetry *The Magic Nest* and *I Am Wings: Poems About Love*.